Collectible
Blue and White
Stoneware

by

Kathryn McNerney

COLLECTOR BOOKS
P.O. Box 3009
Paducah, KY 42001

The current values in this book should be used only as a guide. They are not intended to set prices, which vary from one section of the country to another. Auction prices as well as dealer prices vary greatly and are affected by condition as well as demand. Neither the Author nor the Publisher assumes responsibility for any losses that might be incurred as a result of consulting this guide.

Additional copies of this book may be ordered from:

Collector Books
P.O. Box 3009
Paducah, KY 42001

@$9.95 Add $1.00 for postage and handling.

Copyright: Kathryn McNerney, 1981
Values Updated

This book or any part thereof may not be reproduced without the written consent of the Author and Publisher.

Printed by IMAGE GRAPHICS, Paducah, Kentucky

Appreciation

We were welcomed by these intensely dedicated and friendly collectors in photographing the old pieces that have become their today's treasures . . . and we could never forget the coffee (and doughnuts) that made us feel "right at home" after driving at all hours in all kinds of weather.

Alan Harris	Ozark, Missouri
Back Door Antiques	Losantville, Indiana
Blair's Antiques	Murfreesboro, Tennessee
Court Square Antiques	Murray, Kentucky
Helena C. Parker	Albion, Illinois
Immigrant Trail Antiques	Murfreesboro, Tennessee
Judy Stroud	La Vergne, Tennessee
Ken and Mary Hudgens	Hermitage, Tennessee
Mary Walls	Lake City, Kentucky
Melba Mertz	McLeansboro, Illinois
Mrs. Prentice Shockley	Mayfield, Kentucky
Randy Farmer	Princeton, Kentucky
Roadside Antiques	Washington, Indiana
Sharon Fisher	Youngstown, New York
The Donald Feldmeiers	Huntingburg, Indiana

For

Becky Anne
Sharon Again
and
Patsy Too

Photography by
Tom McNerney

Contents

Introduction

Stoneware Pottery in its own time was part of every household, performing so many basic functions it was simply taken for granted. It was made to fulfill a specific need . . . the rapid turning out of masses of inexpensive utilitarian pieces, not for "fancy looks", but for hard daily usage, affordable for purchase by "ordinary folks". Business began to decline around 1875 with the gradual advent of glass and tin for preserving foods, and the growth of home refrigeration and chilled transportation. By 1910 the ware was no longer necessary as originally intended, produced, however, as such until 1920-30.

Clay is universally found, generally suitable for some type of pottery. And "pottery" broadly covers a vast range of clay-based articles, including Saltglazed Stoneware (the traditional Rhineland pottery since the 1500's, known in England from the 1670's); while the term "crockery" refers to glazed earthen or stoneware objects intended for home usage. This book is primarily concerned with Saltglazed Stoneware Domestic Vessels once made in the United States from the latter 1800's into the earlier 1900's . . . mold-fashioned.

A very hard non-porous paste, stoneware is less opaque than earthenware and finer porcelains. When cleared of roots, moss, etc., it resulted in whiter pieces, and clays containing still other impurities also affected color tones, and had slighter heat resistance. Too, certain clays, Illinois for instance, contributed a yellowish tint. But few items ended up purely white without even a faint grayish cast. To say "Blue and Grayish White" is really more accurate, but since the classification of "Blue and White" has for so long been understood, that designation is continued herein.

Under kiln firing at extreme heat (2,200 degrees F.) this common (raw or green) clay flowed together (vitrified), forming a glassy-like surface. Warmed common table salt was thrown into the kiln at peak temperatures, vaporizing over the stacked forms, making a shiny transparent glaze. According to the textures of the clay and the salt, the combined fusing might result, not in the desired fairly smooth clear surface, but in an "orange peel" effect, easily seen as the fruit's skin, or felt by rubbing with the thumb. (Less common Ash Glaze was found in the South, although Texas was more typical, much used there from before the Civil War into the 1920's, a finish of alkali-rich wood ashes mixed with fine-grained clay; Cinder Ash is attributed to the Midwest, leaving a rougher residue with tiny sharp-pointed haphazardly-spaced bumps.) Earlier stoneware was not glazed, strong in itself after firing. Where salt could not reach into deep interior, as steins, tall vases, and so on, a combination of fine-grained clay and water known as "slip" (slurry) could be brushed onto the raw clay to coat the difficult places, much as we ice a cake, glazing to a natural finish.

Glazing sealed the clay, preventing oozing and leaking, liquids were safe indefinitely. It was impervious to acids. Edibles weren't tainted, (an advertising gimmick exploited by one company which declared that foods in their stoneware were never subjected to the "acidy tastes and odors" imparted by storing them in tin and other metal containers). In homes, inns, taverns, restaurants, and stores, fruits, vegetables, jams, jellies, puddings, pickles, pastries, catsup, kraut, cider and vinegar . . . any foodstuffs in stoneware "held". It kept beer and whiskey, milk and water stayed sweet and cool. By the 1870's salt-glazed stoneware ranked equally with topmost wood (barrels, kegs, churns, etc.) in food storage reliability.

And now in our own time stoneware domestic vessels are no longer taken for granted, regarded, instead, as a vigorous symbol of a more robust homelife some years back.

Blue has ever been a favorite decorating color in pottery, first with the original buyers, just as appealing today with collectors. Luckily, cobalt (blue) was one of the few compounds able to withstand such firing intensities. One factor, along with depths of color applications and workmanship, causing in-numerable natural variances in shadings, was that clays differed in original composition from one region to another, no two batches having identical response to firing. For a special order, a potter might have finer-grained clay hauled in to mix with his coarser variety, a costly procedure. Decorating could be done before firing (underglaze) or after firing (overglaze). From degrees of skill in freehand brushing, artists/decorators tried florid Spencerian flourishes and low relief figures. Impressed before firing, cog wheel - or punched - patterns were plentiful, explaining some of the puzzling small overall background squares, centered dots, stars, and such. After 1860 larger factories adopted stencils for rapidity and cost-cutting. (Nineteenth century Southern potters never fully accepted the elaborateness of the Northeast, preferring only "occasional" decorating.) Wheels on which pieces revolved made continuing bands, usually at the top and/or bottom, with or without a design between. Bits of blue were daubed under and inside spouts, below handles, and on top of knobs. Where quality control was practiced, it was good. Fads, of course, came along, one called "Folkarty", ultra-Victorian, fading soon after 1900 in the face of growing machine-work. Interiors received extra-heavy glazes, brushed away over shallow-embossed patterns on the exterior until only bare stoneware peeked through in spots, attractive if properly done. Also called "Brushware" along with "Stoneware", the outside glaze was for appearance only, and without the thick inside glazing, moisture could have leaked through from the inside (oozed) when the piece was being used. Thus, patterns were incised (impressed), stamped, printed, imprinted, traced, stenciled, and embossed (raised), steadily improving, for with experience came expertise. But at no time was this

7

saltglazed stoneware domestic production overall considered skillful art pottery . . . it had no need to be.

Stoneware was far more adaptable to factory than to individual potter's usages. European wares were essential here from our first settlements, native attempts making small progress. Freed of English restrictions after the War of 1812, our potters were enabled to successfully compete with imports. New Jersey had already pioneered; from the east coast this fast-branching industry raced westward into clay-rich Illinois, Indiana, and Iowa, quickly rose in the South and Southwest, finally active from Florida across to the west coast and up into Oregon, the Ohio Valley prominent. Missouri was our outpost supplying most of the kitchen crockery to states farther west as Kansas and the Dakotas, Nebraska with a few makers of its own, until the expanding railroads began bringing in cheaper stoneware, ruining that trade. Western Mountain States moved more slowly, not from lack of the right raw materials but because of sparser-customer-population; larger factories remained in the East and Midwest.

Literally thousands of small kilns dotted the whole country, some installations combining into larger ones; those less adaptable to new ideas fell by the wayside; fire and bankruptcy took their toll. For years many potteries were sold and resold, those still in operation catering to modern trends. Others continued into fourth and fifth generations of one family.

Products sold in a rather limited hundred-mile radius, unless movable kilns stood at waterways. (The high firing tempreatrues required more, however, than the average movable earthernware furnaces could stand.) "Groundhog" kilns were peculiar to Arkansas and portions of the South (Georgia) into the 1900's, but most manufacturers employed the massive ironbound firebrick or stone kilns. Cities as Pittsburgh, Zanesville, East Liverpool, Cincinnati, and Louisville, among many, used boats on the larger connecting rivers, shipping as far as New Orleans. However, even beyond the turn of the twentieth century, various Ohio potters still sold much of their production by peddlers going door to door through the countryside.

When filling customers' job lot orders incorporating advertising (names, types of business, locations, mottoes), the potter's own name or other maker's identification was rarely added. Advertising marks can increase the value of an otherwise somewhat ordinary object; a date is the ultimate! Firms as The Larkin Company, Feed & Grain Stores, Hardware and General Emporiums, and Dairies gave this ware as premiums, while Minnesota and other Milling Companies put them into filled sacks for the same reason.

Only about one-tenth of kiln-stacked pieces were marked; about one percent carried advertising. Many potters failed to mark anything. Despite

8

huge numbers of potters, their uncertain business lifespans, and the many dubious marks that were added, we can make a start at desired identification by observing characteristics perhaps traceable to an area, as the brilliantly blue tulips of Pennsylvania - and its "Dutch" designs - also attributable to parts of Ohio.

A piece with normal age and wear signs with a good full pattern in strong color is far better than one damage-free more crudely molded and/or having sparser, paler color treatment. It must be emphasized that despite the considerable strength of this type domestic ware, it still was not wholly resistant to chips (flakes) and cracks resulting from the casual handling it received in busy households. While perfect examples are, of course, always desirable (and they are around, as evidenced in this book), it is impractical to reject less expensive lightly imperfect ones if you are buying exclusively for your own enjoyment. Even those with greater injuries can have that side turned to the shelf wall, or be treated to an overflow-bouquet. Buying for resale is more selective.

The ware being made in molds, note the two-part mold marks often very clear at the sides, or on such pieces as large pitchers of bulbous or other contours where top and bottom sections are joined at the middle. For articles to be lifted and/or carried about, handles were "pulled" into shape (as were many spouts and pouring lips) as part of the main form for added strength; those to be applied to the main form were molded separately from the body molds; handles were plain, lined, designed, or rope-twisted (two or three pieces of cylindrical clay twisted together to fashion a rope). Coffee Pots (and a few Tea Pots) had attached narrow bottom caps of thinly rolled sheet iron to further preserve their bases against heat exposure, those with only a discolored ring on the pottery have lost the caps. Pots must have been set in, then the metal folded up to fit tightly over the form. Both type pots have keepers molded right into the body just below the inside rims to twist-hold lids being held at pouring tilts, also making a tighter lid-fit to keep the contents hot. Removable clay covers originally protected contents of jam and honey pots, some butter and salt jars (crocks), and the like. Where these had been broken or just disappeared through the years, there are often carefully fashioned wood (mostly maple) tops with self or china (porcelain) finials (knobs) as replacements, acceptable with most collectors. Heavy wire bails (handles) are often restored, and sometimes the original or a re-carved handgrip thereon at center. It is usually better to allow minor deterioration "as is" than make unprofessional repairs, even then not disturbing normal age and wear imperfections, unless you are keeping the piece and personally prefer the "touching up". Freshening any blue pattern is too glaringly apparent. There is little or no crazing on most saltglazed stoneware due to its hard consistency. (Crazing is a network of minute lines in a glazed surface, more often seen on objects made of soft paste and in furniture finishes).

Stated dimensions may vary in acutality from a half to one inch. Spouts and lips are part of top "D." - diameters; "H" is to the tops of knobs; "L." is length. It is interesting that several potters following the same pattern (using good clean molds), dimensions, and color balances carefully laid out, would almost always end up with all sorts of variations in all three phases, not only from their own kilns, another confusion in identification if unmarked.

Pictured here are authentic old pieces in good, fine, or mint condition. This fact weighted importantly with our knowledgeable collectors in their determination of values, along with their active contacts in following todays' market trends. (Each,however, is realistic enough to have at some time or other accepted the less-than-perfect object, continuing vigilant for "trading up".) Amounts set by owner-dealers reflect generally prevailing prices, no downturn nor appreciable abundance of wares anticipated (although here and there dramatic increases seem to have become a more normal escalation in prices). This stoneware can be found - it just takes "looking for" - and there are many beginning collectors. From time to time fine and extensive collections are being offered for sale, usually widely advertised, many of them sold by the individual piece.

Customarily, serious collectors as these adhere strictly to the specific type items in their fields of interest when buying for their collections. The exception in the predominantly blue and white category herein was their additional inclusion of SPONGEWARE articles. None of these pieces was supposed to achieve absolute aesthetic elegance but some of them come pretty cloes to at least a portion of that . . . and overall they encompass "everyday" useful ware. Thus, we, too, are pleased to include them.

SPONGEWARE is of intriguingly uncertain origins, thought to have first appeared in England and America from the 1815-1820's. While our collectors chose only the blending blues and whites with several multicolors, it does carry most other colors, purple rarely. In varied combinations are browns, oranges, blues, and greens; yellow bases are splashed with green; occasional reds, navy blues and infrequent blacks appear. Red Wing, Minnesota potters were well known for their innovations; Wisconsin, Iowa, Ohio, and Illinois contributions were outstanding.

"Spongeware" means the style of decorating, not the clay composition. Forms were washed in a clear alkaline solution. Sponges (and like materials) saturated with paint - and brushes dipped into colors - were applied in "touching" the clay shapes.

Used with few changes over more than a century as a household mainstay (support), Saltglazed Stoneware Domestic Vessels now hold a respected collectible position never imagined by their makers . . . nor their users.

Decorating

Birdbath, Bird and Branch. $700.00-750.00. H. 27″, D. Bowl 18″ Pedestal was shaped in three separate molds, so accurately recessed that each fit perfectly into the other, an ornamental blue ring disguising the two vertical sections.

Vase, Cone. $75.00-85.00. H. 8½″, D. 4″. Collectors vary to its original intent . . . a hanging vase as here, fit into a wall bracket, a cemetery flower holder, or set upright in reverse (the point at the top) with a cone of string inside, the end of the cord pulled through the hole seen at the rim.

Cooking and Serving

BOWLS and CROCKS . . . Kitchen Bowls were made in graduated sizes to nest for space-saving, firing, easier pantry storage, and to accomodate assorted foods. Crocks (Pantry Jars) sold by the pounds they held, not gallons. There is often a top double ring for string-tying a protective cover, this popularized them as Milk Crocks. Those having iron bails (handles) with wood center handgrips were considered "Stovetop Pieces", advertised as "Stewing Pans" or "Cooking Pots". Flat-bottomed crocks could transfer a lot of heat on the old wood/coal cookstoves (ranges). Kiln stacking was done with the smallest piece at the bottom, the largest at the top - if shapes permitted. Stacks of uniform size crocks could reach fifty to a hundred. Recessed lids or those held flush at body rims by their drop-flanges could be fired with the body, as long as finials were stubby "button" knobs; taller they might rock or stick to a piece set on top. Northstar Stoneware Company of Red Wing, Minnesota fired lids separately from crock bodies.

The next two pictures in pale blues show a full set of nesting size BOWLS; following are two in deeper blues - a partial set; good examples of color and detail variations between separate makers (or the same potter) using the same pattern.

Ringsaround (Wedding Ring) Bowls. $395.00 full set of six. Add a minimum $10.00 each - if individually priced.

Sizes:
H. 2½", D. 5"	H. 3½", D. 7"
H. 3", D. 5½"	H. 3¾", D. 7¾"
H. 3", D. 6"	H. 4", D. 8"

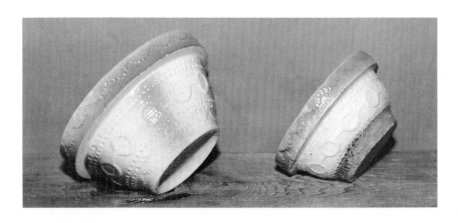

$375.00-385.00. For the set of five. Add about $10.00 each minimum if sold separately. Sizes here include two of the H. 4″,

OD. 8″, the H. 3¾″, D. 7¾″, and the smallest is H. 3½″, D. 7″.

Bowl, Feathers. $135.00-150.00. H. 5½", D. 10½". Double ring for string tying. Mixing bowl.

Bowl, Gadroon Arches (or Petal Panels). $125.00-145.00. H. 4½", D. 9½". Mixing or Dough Bowl; note size irregularities in rim collar design.

Bowl, Diamond Point. $135.00-150.00. H. 5½", D. 10½". Lower section resembles a sunburst; for bread dough; mixing.

Bowl, Reverse Pyramids and Reverse Picket Fence. $100.00-135.00. Mixing bowl, without the picket fence design in reverse, it would be a low figure of about $85.00. The Ruckels Stoneware Company, Monmouth, Illinois originated these upside down fence on rim collars.

Bowl, Currants and Diamonds. $95.00-110.00. H. 5″, D. 9½″. Piecrust rim.

Bowl, Wildflower. $75.00-80.00. H. 4½″, D. 7″. Stencil design and blue rim; rickrack bands underglazed top and bottom.

Flying Bird (Mixing) Bowl. $95.00-110.00 - hard wear. H. 5″, D. 7½″.

Berry Bowl. $50.00-55.00. Diffused Blues. H. 2½″, D. 4½″.

15

Berry Bowl, Cosmos. $55.00-75.00. H. 2½″, D. 4¾″. Beaded medallions; waffle weave background.

Berry/Cereal Crock, Flying Bird. $85.00-95.00. H. 2″, D. 4″.

Berry/Cereal Bowl, Pale Blue Band. $50.00-55.00. H. 2″, D. 4″.

Two Bowls, **Reverse Pyramids** with Ruckels Company's **Reverse Picket Fence. H.** 2½″, D. 4½″ **$95.00-115.00**; H. 5″, D. 7½″ **$55.00-75.00.** Both deeply blue, glazed same color inside and outside.

16

Three **Apricots** with **Honeycomb Crocks**:
a. H. 5″, D. 10″ **$95.00-115.00**.

b. H. 5″, D. 10″ **$95.00-125.00**. **Milk Crock** as well as a **Stovetop Piece**; restored bail and grip.

c. H. 5", D. 10" **$65.00-75.00**. Palest of blues; bail missing.

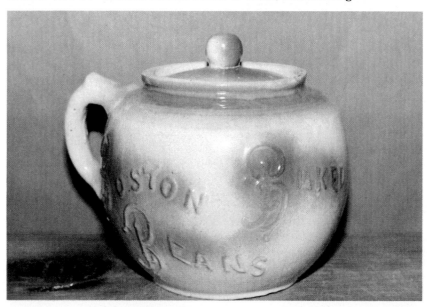

Two **Boston Baked Beans Crocks (Pots)**. (Both lettered two sides).
a. **Swirl** pattern. H. 9", D. 10" widest part. **$195.00-225.00**. Ball finial on recessed lid held by shelf rest on the pot; Spencerian flourishes on capital letters; handle spur.

a. **Swirl** pattern. H. 9″, D. 10″ widest part. **$195.00-225.00**. Ball finial on recessed lid held by shelf rest on the pot; Spencerian flourishes on capital letters; handle spur.

b. **Swirl** - heavier diffused pattern. **$195.00-225.00**. H. 9″, D. 10″ widest part. Acorn finial on same type recessed lid; extra step-up to rim top.

Bowl, Incised Lines $75.00-85.00. H. 4½″, D. 8″. wire bail missing.

Butter Crock. $75.00-85.00. Diffused Blues. H. 4″, D. 4½″. 1 lb. capacity; never had a lid.

Berry Crock, Fluted.
$85.00-95.00. H. 3", D. 4".

Crock used for **Eggs Storage, Barrel Staves.** $175.00-185.00. H. 5½", D. 6". Glaze-worn dots and dashes with blue between.

Milk Crock, Lovebird. Same both sides. **$125.00-145.00.** Restored bail and handgrip. H. 5½″, D. 9″. (One collector remarked: they "look like parakeets")

Two **Daisy** and **Lattice (Milk) Crocks.**
a. **$98.00-115.00.** H. 4″, D. 8″. Good color, little wear.
b. **$65.00-75.00.** H. 5″, D. 10″. Hard usage, pale.

Pastry Crock (or butter), Draped Windows. $200.00-225.00. H. 8″, D. 9″.
Flower finial; note yellowish tinge and that the pale blue over the yellow
looks greenish. Fruit cake could be stored herein, wrapped in brandy-soaked
cheesecloth to "cure" well in advance of a holiday. Advertised by a Minnesota Potter who stressed its economical advantages for thus preserving
foods to keep them "fresh".

Pickle Crock.
$135.00-150.00. H. 12″, D.
9″. Advertising "Dodson &
Braun's Fine Pickles, St.
Louis". **Blue Band.** Recessed
lid with flat knob.

Pickle Crock, Blue Band. $150.00.
H. 12″, D. 9″. Unusual feature is
the extra-long ears for the wire
bail, giving greater strength.

Crock, Advertising.
$75.00-110.00. H. 9½″, D.
8½″. Hirsch's Goodies - could
have held preserves, fruits,
pickles, one of many delicacies.

Pickle Crock. $200.00-225.00.
Heart Band. H. 8″, D. 8″.
Advertising wares; H.J. Heinz Co.,
Pittsburg, U.S.A. Keystone
imprinted - Pickling & Preserving
Works Trademark; heavily rolled
rim; inside brown glaze.

Crock (Jar) Advertising. $95.00-100.00. H. 8", D. 7½" Palest **Diffused Blues**. Icebox container; oversize pulled ears.

Vinegar/Cider Crock, Brushed Leaves. $150.00-175.00. H. 18-19", D. 16" at widest part. Front view; replacement wood lid; "Stippled" background; embossed leaves one side; tiny "3" on other denoting 3-gallon capacity; pulled ears for missing snap-in wire bail; collector indicated Pennsylvania technique.

Coffee and Tea Pots

Both style pots are choice in a collection. Sometimes, in these as other pieces in this field collectors finding a duplicate will "swap". Those not having either item, ever search for them, desiring both their attractiveness and intrinsic worth, for the latter can only increase.

Four **Coffees** have pouring spouts at the top rims, two have lowered spouts, that of the **tea** being long and graceful.

Coffee. Oval. $225.00-250.00. H. 11″, D. 4″. Diffused blues; blue tipped knob, base metal cap missing.

Swirl Coffee. $350.00-425.00. H. 11½″, D. 6″. Color-drips on blue tipped finial (knob); fanciful "Spurs" are convenient hand holds in lifting and pouring; iron base cap.

Oval Coffee. $200.00-225.00. H. 11″, D. 4″. Diffused blues; small diameter of deeply recessed lid inside a raised rim is balanced to overall pot size with a larger and higher finial; metal cap missing.

Swirl Coffee. $350.00-425.00. H. 11½″, D. 5″. This illustrates makers' variances of a same pattern; see page 7; blues are paler, handle narrower than Page 25 Coffee; metal cap is intact - a plus. (Color comparisons can also be seen between the Oval Coffee and that on page 25 - note this oval is indefinite.)

Swirl Tea Pot. $375.00-450.00. H. 9″, D. 6½″. Double wire bail fastened through pulled ears, wire penetrates center wood handgrip; high-relief split balls frame a handsomely-proportioned-pot-to-form highset lid with generous finial.

Swirl Coffee. $375.00-450.00. H. 11½″, D. 6″. Blue acorn finial; metal base; spurred strong handle; large easy-pouring spout.

Cooler Containers

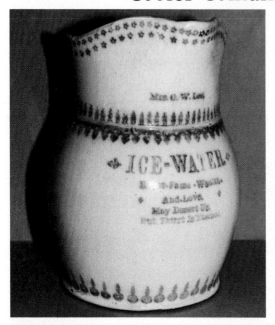

Anniversary Ice Water Pitcher. $350.00-425.00. H. 15″, D. 12″. "ICE WATER Honor-Fame-Wealth-And-Love May Desert Us But Thrift Is Eternal" "Souvenir of Kentucky" on bottom; date inside base. Inside rim also has two star rows; star-line on spur-top, whorlbase applied graceful handle; fanciful bands either side of groove where lower and upper pitcher section molds were joined; still another but blending design around base.

Ice Water Jug, Polar Bear. $395.00-425.00. Up. H. 10″, D. 9¾″. Polar bears, ice floes, seals, and aurora borealis; delicate blues - almost in swirls; applied large spout at a high pouring position; set on an oblong base; two sides identical.

Ice Water Jug, Diffused Blues. $175.00-195.00. H. 7″, D. 7″. Cork affixed inside rounded-thick stopper; another high pouring position spout pulled from the clay body; handle is also at a high position; flat base.

Ice Crock, Barrel Staves. $195.00-225.00. H. 4½″, D. 6″. Rope bands, ice tongs, and ice block; from the latter 1800's; uncommon.

Ice Water Cooler, Apple Blossom. $550.00-650.00. H. 17″, D. 15″. Among the finest of the patterns. Chain and rope bands with design fully repeated on the lid and its blossom finial; unusual fishtail-end handle on a brass turn spigot that has a petal reinforcement in the clay; number "3" (denoting 3-gallon capacity) in a laurel wreath on reverse side.

Water Cooler, Cupid. $575.00-650.00. One of the choice patterns. H. 15″, D. 12″. Cupid has a quiver with arrows and a bow; scrolls at sides, fanciful picture frame and archery repeat-designs top and bottom bands; brass turn spigot; patterned lid with flat finial.

A **Cooler (Dispenser)** is a large cask or jar (crock), with some type of spigot, for cooling and/or serving water, cider, tea, beer, etc., from a counter in a place of business or on a table at home. Putting in a big chunk of ice in the morning (and keeping the lid tight) insured that liquids being poured over the ice as needed would remain cool all day.

Polar Bear Cooler. **$550.00-675.00.** H. 17″, D. 15″. Seals, bears, and Aurora Borealis panorama around Crock; brass nickel plated push spigot; flat recessed finial in lid.

Cooler, Elk and Polar Bear. H. 14″, D. 9½″. **$550.00-600.00** with original lid and spigot. **$375.00-450.00** "as is" without original lid, spigot.

Embossed **Sanitary Water Keg**; elk and trees one side; polar bear standing on its hind legs on the other side; each animal is framed in a medallion (teeth held by twisted rope); imaginative bands top and bottom; diffused blues; carefully fit maple restoration lid.

Iced Tea Cooler, Blue Band. H. 13", D. 11". **$275.00-295.00.** The yelowish tint of the unglazed stacking ring next to the lid's edge was accentuated in film processing, tinging overall what is really a grayish white crock. Imprinted in the lid petals band is "W.3", meaning "Watercolor 3 gallon". The flat "button" lid was developed first, difficult to grasp, so the handle, partial - space beneath followed, an improvement. Red Wing Stoneware Company, Minnesota made the first pushbutton spigot; this "Up" lever (particlarly when pitchers and such larger containers than mugs and glasses were being filled) could be pulled down into a "Hold" position, depressing the spigot button, released again to "Up" when filling was completed. Minnesota's Northstar Stoneware Company used this crossbar-enforced iron handle style that penetrated through pulled heavy ears. A patch of clay, plain or design fashioned, reinforced the spigot drain holes to withstand the punching and turning of permanent metal spigots or the "pounding-in" of wooden ones. This is indeed a fortunate find with complete original features in mint condition.

Ice Water Dispenser, Blue Bands. $150.00-175.00. H. 17", D. 13". Push
spigot.

Beer Cooler, Elves. $550.00-850.00. H. 18″, D. 14″ widest part. Deeply clear embossings - Elves holding steins, making merry in a forest of leaves and scrolls; blue bands; brass turn-spigot with petal decorated blue reinforcement; typically Pennsylvania.

Maxwell House Iced Tea Cooler. $185.00-210.00. H. 15″, D. 13″. Push spigot, square block clay reinforcement; wood top restoration, flat button lift, inside dropped ring to fit inside rim of body - also typical of the stoneware lids.

Cider Cooler. $250.00-275.00. H. 15″, D. 13″ widest part. Motto: "Good To The Core"; handy larger knob; attributed to the Ohio Valley's Logan Pottery Company; squared clay reinforces wood turn-spigot.

Syrup Dispenser, Pep-So. $300.00-325.00. H. 12″, D. 9″. Original metal lid replaced with clay blue lattice pattern and mushroom knob. A shot of Pep-So syrup in a glass followed by fizz water was a popular drink at soda fountains. **Coolers** are also knowns as **Fountains**.

Johnston Cold Fudge Crock. $225.00-250.00. H. 13″, D. 12″. Wood knob, tinned lid and dipper; customary at soda fountains - over ice cream.

Cups and Tumblers

Cup, Bowtie with Bird Transfer, shallow relief (raised). **$75.00** minimum. H. 3¾", D. 3½".

Cup, Paneled Fir Tree. $75.00 minimum. H. 3½", D. 3". Spurs on applied handle.

Crock, Sample size Advertising. **$45.00** minimum. H. 3", D. 4½". Missing wire bail.

Cup, Wildflower with Embossed Ribbon and Bow. $75.00-85.00 minimum. H. 4½", D. 2½".

Cup, Custard. $75.00. H.
5″, D. 2½″. **Fishscale**; not
too many available.

Tumbler, Diffused Blues.
$65.00-75.00 H. 6″, D. 3″.

Jars and Jugs

Cookie Jar, Brickers. $295.00. H. 8″, D. 8″ at widest part. Very desirable
piece; deeply recessed lid with flat button finial. The jar held hard little tea
cookies called "Bricks", a Pennsylvania preference. It is, then, natural to
begin maker-identification in that State.

41

Cookie Jar, Grooved Blue. $95.00-110.00. H. 8", D. 7¼". Without the original lid, it is still a fine piece in mint condition; lid would add about $15.00.

Cookie Jar. $175.00-195.00. H. 9", D. 8″ widest part Acorn finial; "Turkey Eye" color drip; deep diffused color bands.

Three **Flying Bird** objects, the design a collectors' favorite. Left: **Grease Jar.** $210.00-260.00. Center: **Cookie/Biscuit Jar.** $325.00-350.00. H. 9″, D. 6¾″. Without original lid would be about $250.00-275.00; Right: **Bowl** (here contains eggs). $175.00-195.00 H. 3½″, D. 6½″.

Batter Jar, Wildflower. H. 8″, D. 7″ $175.00-195.00. Thick applied handle a bit whiter than body form; pinched (as in piecrust thumb and fingers position) spout neatly directs batter onto a griddle; top of handle offset from bulbous jar's side mold line. **Batter jars,** usually holding one gallon, were used for both mixing and pouring hotcakes batter. Being so utilitarian, they were mostly left plain - but decorated in just about any design - even blue-swabbed briefly at handle and below spout - or as here with a bold blue band, blue-edged rim, and stenciled wildflowers, they are especially fine. The earliest were made from heavier-than-average-clay . . . and this is exactly that.

Batter (Pail or Crock), Basketweave and Flower. $125.00-145.00. H. 7″, D. 8″. Rim extends into tiny pinched spout. Handle holes do not penetrate through the clay body, this to insure no possible rusting of the iron gets into the batter.

Beater Jar, Blue Bands, Advertising. $75.00-95.00 H. 5″, D. 5½″. Wood handle-held wire beaters could be easily whirled around on rounded interior base; easy to wash clean. From the Red Wing Union Stoneware Co., Red Wing, Minnesota (1906-1930). One of their "famous" jars.

Wesson Oil Jar. $65.00-75.00. H. 5″, D. 5″. Rounded bottom inside and usage as in the Red Wing Beater Jar; Printed: "For Making Good Things To Eat".

Mustard Jar (pot), Strawberry. $65.00-85.00. H. 4″, D. 3″. Base maked: Robinson Clay Pottery Co., Akron, Ohio. With lid the value would be about $20.00 more.

Lard. $95.00-125.00. H. 5″, D. 5″. Restored handle; set-on-rim-lid; snap-in bail ends.

Diffused Blues, two jars, (Crocks, Pails). **Refrigerator. $95.00-125.00. H. 6″, D. 6″.** Recessed lid; large hook-through ears.

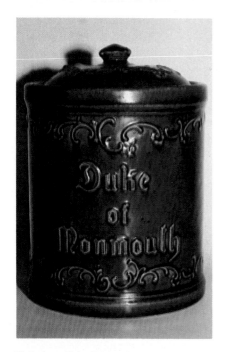

Tobacco Jar, Berry Scrolls.
$175.00-225.00. H. 6½", D. 5".
Deeply blue with highlights;
ornate; DUKE OF MONMOUTH
one side, M.C.C. Co. other; lid
vent has a cork; mushroom finial,
base date is 1905.

Brandy Jug, Hunting Scene.
$375.00-385.00. H. 8", D. 4"
widest part. All-around-Jug hunting
scene panorama with dog and hare
activity in mountainous terrain;
beading; floral patterns; from a Pennsylvania Potter in the latter 1800's.

Planter Jug, Diffused Blues. $65.00-75.00. H. 4½", D. widest part 3".
Unusual piece
Miniature Crock. $75.00-85.00. Missing bail that snapped-under ears pulled
from rim clay. H. 2", D. 4"

46

Measures and Holders

Measuring Pitcher. $75.00-85.00. H. 8½", D. 7". Half gallon capacity; pulled handle unseen at the rear; nice wide pouring fence.

Measuring Cup. $110.00-115.00. H. 6", D. 6¾". **Spearpoint and Flower Panels.** Top spur handle, rather narrow handhold space.

Swan Toothpick Holder. $55.00-65.00. H. 3¼″, D. 4″. Duck Match Holder. $75.00. H. 5″, D. 5½″. Held the long old-fashioned sulphur matches. Measuring Cup. $100.00-115.00. H. 5¾″, D. 6½″. slightly varying dimensions and handle shaping from this same design cup on page 56, Spearpoint and Flower Panels.

Mugs

Each side: Diffused Blues Mug. $95.00-100.00. H. 5½″, D. 3½″. Center: Flying Bird Mug. $135.00-150.00. H. 5″, D. 3″ Petals band top and bottom.

Flying Bird Mixing Bowl. $175.00-195.00. H. 4″, D. 7½″.

Flying Bird Mug. $145.00-170.00. H. 5″, D. 3½″. Deeper blues' brilliance increases value.

Basket Weave and Flower Mug. $95.00-125.00. H. 5″, D. 3″. Roped square-top handle, bulbous at bottom tapering to a rim roll; delicately diffused blues.

Windy City Mug. $175.00-195.00. (Also called **Fannie Flagg**). H. 5½″, D. 3¼″. These are rarely marked as is this one: "The Robinson Clay Pottery Co., Akron, Ohio". Double beading rows below rim. See description of Pitcher in this design Page 86.

Beer Mug, Flemish and Buffalo. $125.00-150.00. H. 5″, D. 3″. Burghers Drinking Scene one side, Western Plains Buffalo other side; beading and lines on extra-large squared easy-lift handle; background cog wheel curves; blue brushed over raised figures.

Advertising Mug. $200.00-225.00. H. 5″, D. 3¼″. Four embossed bands; marked: "WSCo." (Western Stoneware Company, Monmouth, Illinois Est. 1870).

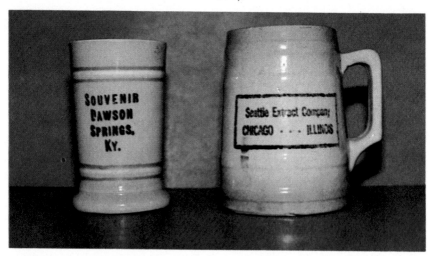

Advertising Mugs. $45.00-50.00. Souvenir Dawson Springs, Ky. H. 4½″, D. 2½″. Has a conventional handle; turned so advertising is seen; yellowish tint in clay; blue bands; one usage could have been a chocolate cup. **Beer Mug**, Seattle Extract Company, Chicago, Illinois. **$75.00-100.00.** H. 5″, D. 3½″. Handle squared only at base; printing; diffused pale blues.

Scuttle Mug, Diffused Blues. $325.00-425.00. H. 6″, D. 4″. A FAD made here in limited quantities after the Civil War into the turn of the century, it was a shaving accessory whose name stemmed from its similar appearance to old European coal scuttles. In two components, the top for soap (usually round bars) and the lower for water, later examples have top section drainholes to allow moisture (lather) to drip off the soap into the lower part. The large round spout is for pouring in hot water before shaving, for dipping off the water after usage . . . and for handily storing the shaving brush.

Pie Plates

Bottom views; unglazed under the lip edges. **Pale Blue. $95.00** minimum. X center. D. 9″. Raised broken circles - plain or design-raised bases seen on most backing plates as these. **Blue Walled Brick-Edge** base $100.00 minimum. Center impressed STAR typical of Star Stoneware Co., Akron, Ohio - marked: PATENTED, Dia. 10½″.

Deep Blue X center; **$100.00** minimum. D. 10½". Cinder ash glaze.

Table Pitchers

Butterfly Pitcher. $195.00-225.00. H. 9", D. 7". Heavy orange peel; raised rope medallion surrounds large butterfly; diffused blues emphasize smaller butterflies at top and bottom between raised rope bands.

Bluebird Pitchers. $195.00-250.00 each. Each H. 9″, D. 7″. From separate collections. Same design both sides; not too many available.

Left: Navy with highlights; sharp spur handle molded and then applied over faint body mold line; generous lip.

Right: Lighter but good blues; small lip flake

Alternate sides of the highly desirable **Flying Bird Pitcher**. On one, two larger birds perch on a thickly-foliaged branch, several smaller background-white birds overhead. The other side has about four birds of varying sizes in flight. At top and base all around the pitcher is a grass and flower (lilies of the valley) border; the low-spur separately molded underglaze beaded handle has a crack-line-break just above the spur as well as a small lip flake, neither too detrimental in view of the pattern and its brilliant color.

Flying Bird Pitcher. $275.00-300.00. H. 9″, D. 6″. Flared; extra clay to more securely hold the handle top.

Flying Bird Pitcher.
$275.00-300.00. H. 9″, D.
6″. Reversed side.

Flying Bird Pitcher.
$275.00-290.00. H. 9″, D.
6″. Flared; narrower spout;
lip roughness.

Rare **Flying Bird Pitcher and Mug Set. $450.00** (and could go to $600.00 in some locales) for the seven pieces. H. 9″, D. 6″ Pitcher. H. 4½″, D. 3″ each mugs. One dealer commented the set is "priceless". Slightly flared top and base. Spurs are at the top of the Mug handles, near the base of the pitcher's.

Peacock Pitcher. $275.00-325.00 dependent upon area and circumstances; rarely less in value. H. 7¾″, D. 6½″. Royal Palms and Berries with Fountains; brick walk and beading rings; front body mold line roughness is treated as a column with pulled-out spout embossings; this pattern rarely other than delicate blue tones; **Peacock** ranks among the most desirable of all designs. **Peacock Salt Crock (Jar). $265.00-325.00.** Complete; mint condition; unglazed inside-crock brief shelf just below rim supports recessed lid.

Three **Lovebird Pitchers.** Each side carries the birds on a branch mirror-framed in grooves and beading. H. 8½", D. 5½" for all; deeper colors always a "plus"; not a pattern seen with regularity, and sought by collectors. Palest, wear roughness, $135.00-165.00; Deeper color, top and bottom curling bands, $185.00-210.00; Deepest color, arc bands top and bottom with center dots, mint conditon, $265.00-280.00.

Two **Swan Pitchers.** Both H. 8½", D. 5½". Each has same design both sides - leaf and flower medallions framing swans on water; curled top bands; leaves at bases; beaded handles.

Faintly blue, peacefully swimming swan. **$150.00-175.00.**

Deeper but soft blues; longer-beak bird; with ruffled feathers and high-arched neck it seems ready to dart at a bug. **$175.00-195.00.**

Stag and Pine Trees Pitcher. $175.00-225.00. H. 9″, D. 6½″. Forceful fewer details dominate each side; faintly yellowish but enough to make the blue seem greenish-blue; a longer than usual handle with spurred, squared top; there are other sizes.

Doe and Fawn Pitcher. $165.00-185.00. H. 8½″, D. 6″. Again, sparse but strongly embossed detail; Doe standing under a blossoming tree as her Fawn rests in the grass; bulbous base having graceful scroll. **Leaping Deer.** **$155.00-165.00.** H. 8½″, D. 6″. Leaf medallion.

Cow Pitcher. $175.00-195.00. H. 8½″, D. 6″. Cows framed in rope and bead medallion; beads overall; roped handle; any authentic collectible in all categories having cows' designs are desirable. **Leaping Deer.** **$100.00-115.00.** H. 8½″, D. 6″. Base rope band; hard usage.

Pitcher, Cherry
Cluster.
$165.00-185.00. H.
7½", D. 6¼". Bead
center squares overall;
leaf bands top and
bottom; tiny spur near
base of applied blue-
daubed handle; flared
rim and base.

Pitcher, Cherry Cluster and Basketweave. $145.00-155.00. H. 10", D.
8½". Grooved bands. Pitcher, Apricot. $135.00-160.00. H. 8", D. 6½".
Base wear; chain medallion; fanciful body design of leaves and twigs with
a roped handle -pattern carried onto spout.

61

Cherries and Leaves Pitchers . Two views of a universally famous design from the Red Wing Union Stoneware Company of Red Wing, Minnesota (1906-1930), its deeply cut lines and clean shapes evidence of new molds. Overall the carefully executed pattern turned out pretty much the same on both pitchers. On the pitcher without advertising, the spur-top squared handle has shrunk slightly since being applied, but through age, and on such a distinctive rarity, no value deterrant. The very large pulled spouts assure easy pouring with little drippage. H. 9½", D. 6". **$275.00-300.00** with printing.

"Compliments of
H.R. SOULE,
Strictly a Store For The People
ADAIR, IOWA"
H. 9½", D. 5½". **$200.00-225.00** without printing.

A set of seven pieces and two single Pitchers, **Grape with Leaf Band**, Uhl Pottery Co., Huntingburg, Indiana, all having waffle square backgrounds. **Pitcher and Six Mugs Set. $475.00-550.00.** Set of 7 Pcs. Pitcher: H. 9½", D. 5½"; Mugs, each: H. 5", D. 3½". Comfortable handlegrips on the mugs.

Paler blue. **$125.00-150.00.** H. 9", D. 5".

A different color treatment; daubed-on diffused. **$125.00-150.00.** H. 9", D. 5".

Grape Cluster On Trellis Pitchers. $525.00-600.00 set of four. H. 9½″, D. 7½″; H. 8½″, D. 6½″; H. 7″, D. 5½″; H. 5″, D. 4″. Top and bottom leaf stars bands; maker: Uhl Pottery Company, Huntingburg, Indiana.

Grape Cluster on Trellis Pitcher. $135.00-150.00. H. 7″, D. 7″. Same pattern and maker as Set of Four Pitchers in same design.

Pitcher, Grape Cluster In Shield. $175.00-225.00. H. 8″, D. 6″. Arrow point bands; beadings; impressed psuedo-wood body. **Pitcher, Wild Rose.** $150.00-175.00. H. 9″, D. 6″. At top is flower, leaf, and stem band; arc and diamond at base.

Pitcher, Grape With Rickrack on waffle background. This design in two color tones. H. 8″, D. 6″. **$100.00-125.00.** White clay; diffused blues.

H. 9″, D. 6″. **$135.00-150.00.** Deeper blues; marked on base: the "Northstar" of Northstar Stoneware Co., Red Wing, Minnesota.

66

Pitcher, Basketweave and Flower (Morning Glory). $175.00-225.00. H. 9″, D. 6½″. Rope-twisted squared-top handle; clean, deep embossings.

Pitcher, Wildflower, stenciled. $175.00-200.00. Blue rim and ring; a heavy homey piece with a big handle . . . probably filled with buttermilk, it was set right on the table - to be passed around from hand to hand.

Pitcher, Rose on Trellis. $125.00-150.00. Only slightly yellowish; bulbous base.

Two Bulbous (Bellied) **Pitchers**, handles set high. **Daisy Cluster.** $175.00-195.00. H. 8″, D. 8″. Rim tulip petals band; decorated handle; lovely color variations. Value could reach $200.00-250.00 with proper area circumstances.

Poinsettia with Square Woven Cane background. $175.00-195.00. H. 6½″, D. 7¾″ widest part. Embossed loosely braided rolls at top, daubed handle.

Iris Pitcher. $145.00-165.00. H. 9″, D. 5½″. Quilted diamond band below flared rim; incurved body.

Old Fashioned Garden Rose. H. 10″, D. 7″. **$150.00-175.00.** Tight-petaled and spicey. **Tulip Pitcher. $145.00-165.00.** H. 8″, D. 4″. Short, chunky handle.

American Beauty Rose Pitcher. $225.00-275.00. H. 10″, D. 7″. Tapered; beadings on low-applied handle and edging embossed rolls; petals around top and bottom.

Wild Rose Pitcher. $250.00-275.00. H. 9″, D. 6½″. Tapered; sponge-touched over roughed-up clay; double beadings; separately molded and applied handle.

Pine Cone Pitcher. $185.00-195.00. H. 9½″, D. 5¾″. Both sides identical pattern; with scarcity, simplistic appeal and demand by a number of collectors, value is increased.

Cattails (Rushes) Pitchers. $125.00-150.00. H. 10", D. 7½". Bulbous, rather small squared handle for body dimensions. H. 9½", D. 6", $100.00-125.00. H. 7½", D. 5¾", $125.00-150.00. Not a common size to find.

Arc and Leaf Paneled Creamer. $65.00-75.00. H. 4½", D. 4". Cattails Pitcher. $100.00-125.00. H. 10½", D. 7½".

Avenue of Trees Pitcher with brilliantly blue designed bands. $125.00-145.00. H. 7", D. 7½". See description of pattern on Page 89.
Printed Acorns Pitcher. $100.00-135.00. H. 8", D. 6½". Applied handle top is interestingly strengthened with a large blob of clay mashed into body rim's squares-and-curls embossed band; front of body mold line is smoothed into the lip, also obliterating the design there.

Avenue of Trees Pitcher.
$125.00-135.00. H. 8", D. 7¾".
Palely blue with curved-in top and base.

Avenue of Trees Pitcher. $175.00-200.00. H. 9″, D. 7″. Excellent color, sharp lines and clear embossings; long handle; Doric type columns; road imprinted with wheel marks terminating at a gate across the far end; motif of arched leaves overhead; rolled-in top with pulled pouring lip. In this, as in glazed stoneware pitchers of many other designs, there are varying sizes, from creamers to big buttermilks.

Pitcher, Windmill and Bush. $175.00-225.00 to area. H. 9″, D. 6″. Bulbous base with tulips all around; pulled lip and handle.

Pitcher, Dutch Children and Windmill. $175.00-200.00. H. 9″, D. 6″. Tulip petals band above incised lines. **Pitcher, printed Dutch Farm.** $175.00-200.00. H. 9″, D: 8″. Bulbous top and bottom with clearcut open blossoms; two figures and a dog; note handle shaping on both pieces in this picture.

Pitcher, Dutch Landscape. $150.00-175.00. Printed scene, Dutch figures, town in distance; distinct handle mold lines.

Next are the reverse side of two **Pitchers** of the same "starter" pattern, two figures each side . . . Pitchers are both . . . H. 6¼″, D. 6¾″. **$250.00-275.00.**

With infinitesimal differences in details and color tones, dependent upon the locale, one of these three names is generally used:

INDIAN BOY AND GIRL, KISSING PILGRIMS, AND
CAPT. JOHN SMITH AND POCAHONTAS

Stories relate that once they were married, the Capt. like to see his wife gowned as here (he bought many of her dresses himself), English schoolgirl types with big sashes and sailor collars, her Indian headdress topping it all. The Capt., if so it be,

wears a frock coat and small stiff hat typical of the period. On one side they are standing apart as though in conversation, on the other he is closely looking into her face.

For the paler blues pitcher, the figures are the same on one side; on the other the Capt. is leaning or half-sitting on a rail fence, not wearing his hat, seemingly chatting with Pocahontas.

Swastika (Greek cross bent at right angles) **Pitcher.** **$175.00-195.00.** (Also called Indian Good Luck Sign) H. 9″, D. 7″. Adopted emblem of the Nazi Third Reich (familiar during World War II); smaller reverse-insignia on bands is the Indian Sign; heavy orange peel.

Indian In War Bonnet Pitcher. **$225.00-250.00.** H. 9″, D. 6½″. Much sought after pattern. Mirror rolls frame Indian on both sides; waffle squares on separately molded applied handle.

Columns and Arches Pitcher. $250.00-295.00. H. 9″, D. 6½″. Among the finest designs; Ionic type Greek Columns supporting arches; brick walled overall background; convex-flared diamond point top band; uncommon handle decorating variation of Greek Cross lines at top of beaded applied handle.

Shield Pitcher. $150.00-175.00. H. 8½″, D. 6″. Two primitive shields within the larger at center with half-shields set at each side; reverse side of pitcher has the same design; minor rim imperfection.

Pitcher, Scroll and Leaf. $175.00-195.00. Small no-harm flakes but spider (crack) down pitcher's side limits pricing. H. 8", D. 7". Advertising for Dows, Iowa Merchant; extra-large pulled pouring lip; whorl-base handle received attention from decorator. (Whorl is the French turned-up or curled "whorl-foot" so admired on Victorian furniture and Chippendale's Louis XV styles.)

Raised **Bands and Rivets Pitcher.** $100.00-115.00. H. 5½", D. 5½".
Tapered **Blue Band Pitcher.** $75.00-85.00. H. 8", D. 6". Pale Narrow
Bands **Pitcher.** $95.00-100.00. H. 8½", D. 6½".

Barrel Staves Pitcher.
$110.00-125.00. H. 7", D.
6''.

Simplicity Pitcher. $65.00-75.00. H. 9", D. 4".
Barely blue.

Following are several pictures of the celebrated **Lincoln Head Pitchers** made by Huntingburg, Indiana's Uhl Pottery Company. While sizes and blue tones vary, the basic design remains the same, the Head of Lincoln continuing on into a soft collar and tie, and a cabin in the trees.

Values may differ regionally, but to no great extent.

Individual sizes and prices of each if sold separately:

H. 10", D. 7"	$450.00 - could be $600.00
H. 8", D. 6"	$325.00
H. 7", D. 5"	$250.00-275.00.
H. 6", D. 4"	$225.00-250.00 - seen in a very pale blue at $150.00 (1981)
H. 4¾", D. 4¾"	$150.00-175.00

Pitcher. $225.00-375.00. From another collection. H. 6″, D. 4″. Small, Pitchers (Creamers). H. 4¾″, D. 4¾″ $175.00. H. 3¼″. D. 3¼″ $175.00.

Monastery (or Castle) and Fishscale Pitcher. Larger . . . H. 9″, D. 7½″, grayish **$195.00-225.00.** Smaller . . . H. 8″, D. 6¾″, whiter **$150.00-175.00.** Slight spur-handle differences but both "different"; of three peaked roofs atop a mountain, the highest has a cross at the lower portion of its tall spire; huge pine tree at front with brick wall/drive leading upward. (There is also a still smaller - creamer - size.)

Windy City Pitcher (or Fannie Flagg). $375.00 - more to locale and cir-
cumstances. Wind is whipping figure with "pompadour" hair and theatrical
clothing appropriate to just before and at the turn of the century on a
downtown street corner (Chicago, Illinois); central design on reverse side
is a tall building; separate building corners; dot-dash top band, street
represented below; branch handle with thumb-brace. Few of these pieces
are marked as here: "The Robinson Clay Pottery Co., Akron, O.". See mat-
ching **Mug** on page 49.

Monk Stein (Pitcher). $375.00-425.00. H. 11.., D. 6″. In one hand the Monk holds a stein, the other tilts a Mug to drink; center (buckle) of all three handles (including Mugs), separately molded and applied, is unusual - affording good finger-firming; blue dabbed spout; center figure on one side only, with medallions design-relating to the handle buckle.

Mugs. $100.00-150.00 each. H. 4½″, D. 3½″. Prominent side mold marks on all three pieces have been rounded, making them part of decorative detail.

Pitcher, Edelweiss. $250.00-275.00. H. 9″, D. 5″. Flower on plain clay
with beading frame and overall background, varied from plain raised dots
with body-color scallops and petals, metal thumb rest also strengthens; "Pro-
sit" a toast (salutation) to good health meaning' "May it do you good"..

Edelweiss Pitcher. $250.00-275.00. H. 8½", D. 4½". (The Edelweiss is a white flowering herb of the aster family, found high in the Alps). Flower each side; rope type bands; scrolled and blue painted spur-top applied handle; drinking salutation to health.

Flemish Figures Pitcher. $475.00-550.00. H. 9½", D. 5½". Seated group on one side may be watching (other side) maid leaning on a keg of beer (ale) having served a richly clad Burgomaster (mayor); top grapes and leaves band; base has band of tulips buds.

Paul Revere Pitcher. $400.00 - and could increase to area to $650.00. H. 7″, D. 7″. Embossed "Paul Revere" depicting him delivering message of coming of the British to a colonist; other side shows defender bidding his parents farewell; related top decorating and bottom harvest motif both sides; psuedo-bark handle conveniently shaped for comfortable holding; intricately detailed designs.

Hunting Scene Pitcher. $295.00-300.00 up. H. 7″, D. 8″ widest part. This type best found among Pennsylvania owners, heavily reflecting old German techniques. Stag at bay on one side; Hunters on the other with a fallen Buck; trees and mountain peak outlines; Bavarian hunting togs; a thoughtfully-large psuedo bark handle for lifting such a heavy pitcher - applied with a generous amount of reinforcing extra clay; note uncommon underspout decorating. (German has to do with good health and companions.)

Bulbous (bellied) **Bavarian Alpine Beer Pitcher. $650.00-750.00.** H. 14″, D. 9″ widest part. On one side a native Climber leans on his staff; the other has a bearded man in native dress looking into the distance; overall is beading (dots); such realistic facial expressions on the men and fine mouth, nose, eyes looking straight ahead, even proper ears, of the mastiff's head fashioned from the reinforcing clay of the snap-in iron and wood handgrip handle; the latter's clay was scrolled to end in a whorl base -blue-lined - and then applied; side mold marks were painted. The German toast (salutation), liberally translated, means "for health and fellowship". Uncommonly, the blued spout was elaborately designed. This interesting Pitcher once carried from Munich, Germany to Mrs. Pauline Tabor Webster, presently of Texas, is the exception to American objects herein, relating through clay composition, technique, color, and design; and because it importantly completes a fine Tennessee collection . . . similars (from parts of Pennsylvania and Ohio) are well worth pursuing.

Roaster and Bakers

Roaster, Diffused Blues. $175.00-195.00 unusual form. H. 9″, Length 19″.
Thick, applied handles; flat finial.

Roaster, Heart and Drapery. No lid $125.00-150.00. With lid
$165.00-200.00. Popular pattern. H. without lid 5″, D. 12″.

Roaster, Grooved Band. $135.00-150.00. H. 9", D. 16".

Roaster, Wildflower. $95.00-125.00. H. 8½", D. 12".

Double Roaster, Chain Link. $125.00-150.00. H. 9″, D. 11″. Top or bottom may be independently used; top has ear handleholds; unglazed rims.
Baker, Chain Link. $95.00-110.00. H. 6½″, D. 7″. Flat button finial.

Rolling Pins (Rollers)

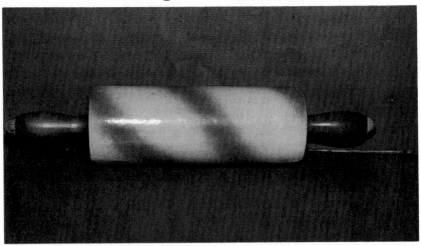

Swirl Roller. $250.00-275.00. Length 13″, Diameter 3″. Original wood handles; most sought after pattern in Rollers.

A collector's **Display Rack of Rolling Pins.** L. approx. 13″ to 15″. D. approx. 3″ to 4½″. **$145.00-175.00 (no adv.). Wildflower and Blue Band** patterns (with **Onion** and **Plain Milkglass** for interest). On top is a miniature deep blue collar **Bowl.** H. 2″, D. 3″. **$75.00.**

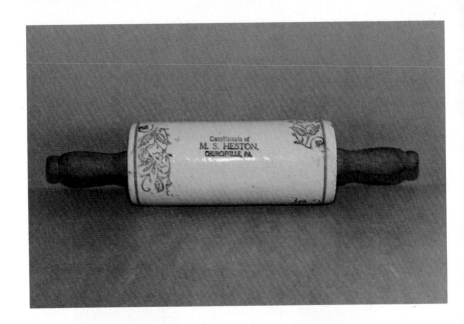

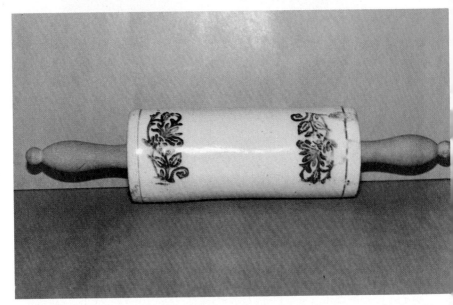

Wildflower Rollers. L. 15", D. 4½" each. With advertising $200.00. Without advertising $150.00. "Compliments of M.S. Heston CHURCHVILLE, PA." Wood handles.

Blue Bands (Advertising) Roller "Dawson Furniture & Hardware Company . . . Zeigler, ILL." $175.00-200.00. Length 14″, D. 4″. (For additional information in that colors on many of these stoneware domestic pieces were not always limited to blues, this same Banded Roller is shown with rust-red lines. The length, diameter, and type of advertising is the same as the Blue Band, here: "ALLAN'S GROCERY etc., in Illinois". In this case, the value was slightly less, being $125.00-150.00. We found that several collectors had purchased such a piece for comparisons, as well as a color accent to blues.

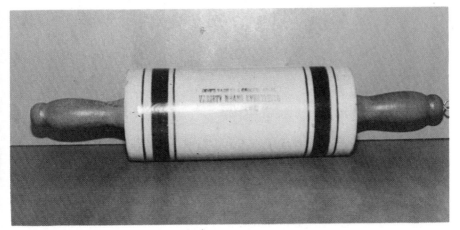

Blue Bands (Advertising) Roller. $175.00-200.00. L. 14″, D. 4″. "Dow's Variety & Grocery Store, VARIETY MEANS EVERYTHING, Dows, Iowa". Original maple handles.

Salt Crocks (Salts)

Long before stoneware and carved wooden saltboxes were known, a household's supply of salt was stored in a deep well cut out under the seat of a "Salt Chair", a custom thought to have originated in Normandy. Sometimes benches had a "Salt Chest" under the seats. Mostly, cooks reached into the Salts by hand and sprinkled the contents over the foods bubbling in pots, a fact which might account for such casual amounts referred to in passed-around-home-recipes as a "pinch" or a "dash" of salt. Salt Crocks have hanging rings fashioned right into the clay. Consequently, they could be hung beside the stove (or set on a shelf provided on the stove itself).

Salt, Apricots at each side in scroll Medallions. **$110.00-125.00.** H. 5", D. 5¾". Lid is missing. Pretty idea for usage.

Salt, Flying Bird. With lid . . . **$265.00-325.00.** Without lid . . . **$200.00-250.00.** H. 6″, D. 6½″. Complete with the original clay lid is, of course, best. Mushroom finial stands high for easy handling; crisscross design on lid.

Salt, Eagle With Arrow In Its Claws. $325.00-375.00. A broken piece of the lid has been reglued, not a severe flaw since no additional clay was added, and more importantly - this is one of the most desirable patterns, not occurring in numbers - but can be found. Note the eagles on each side fly in the same direction; heart scrolls and background impressed dots; roping; a good potter disguised rough side mold marks as decorative vertical bands.

Salt, Apricots in Medallions; brilliant Cobalt (blue). **$125.00-150.00.** H. 5″, D. 5″. **Salt, Peacock** without its original lid **$175.00-195.00.** With original lid **$200.00-250.00.** H. 5″, D. 5″. **Crock, Flying Bird. $225.00-250.00.** H. 9″, D. 6″. For Butter - Biscuits - Pastry Storage.

Two **Salts** having maple replacement lids. **Butterfly.** $125.00-150.00. H. 5¾", D. 5¾". **Apricot.** $125.00-150.00. H. 5", D. 5". Smoothed side mold marks.

Salts, wood replacement lids, one hinged to lift. **Apricot.** $125.00-150.00. H. 5½", D. 5½". **Blackberry.** $135.00-150.00. H. 5½", D. 5½". Deeply cut pattern; not too plentiful.

Salt, Blue Band. $95.00-125.00. Slightly yellow tint; actually more grayish with blue-edged white bands; printed letters. H. 6″, D. 5″.

Salt, Grapevine on Fence. $200.00-225.00. H. 6½″, D. 6¾″. Softly pale diffused color; decorated lid has an unusual liftbar with depressed space on each side, differ from Red Wing Company's in that this solid bar has no open finger space beneath; beading.

Salt, Daisy on Snowflakes. $185.00-225.00. H. 6½″, D. 6″. Crown lid resting on inside-crock rim. Salt, Blocks. $115.00-135.00. H. 6¾″, D. 6½″. Original lid would add about $15.00 more to this piece.

Butter Jars (Crocks)

On many with handles there are the customary "ears", on others the heavy wire bail snaps into the side of the body just halfway through the clay, roughness from the side mold mark evidently considered sufficient reinforcing, simply smoothed or briefly designed.

Low Butter, Grapes and Leaves. $125.00-150.00. H. 3″, D. 6½″. Marked on base: "Robinson Clay Pottery Co., Akron, Ohio" Double ring for string-tying a protective cloth; unglazed rim.

Butter, Diffused Blues. $100.00-115.00. H. 5″, D. 6″. Printed word; original lid has the unglazed ring and flat knob suitable for kiln-stacking.

Butter, Butterfly. $85.00-95.00. H. 6″, D. 10″. Five pound size; missing lid and bail.

Butter, Butterfly. $95.00-110.00. H. 6″, D. 10″. Five pound; restored bail, no handgrip; hard usage.

Butter, Cows and Fence. $250.00-375.00. H. 5″, D. 7¼″. A valuable piece; one cow each front and each reverse side; leaf and cornflower bands; brilliant color; recessed button lid fits securely over unglazed raised ring for holding lid at top of crock body, note . . . as in their natural habitat, the cows are following one behind the other in the same direction all around the crock.

Butter, Cows and Columns. $200.00-225.00. H. 6½", D. 4½". Cows grazing and resting among Egyptian Temple ruins; (knives were honed on this rim); a top pattern.

Butter, Printed Cows. $85.00-95.00. H. 5", D. 6½". Recessed lid missing along with bail from tiny pulled ears.

Butter, Eagle in rarely perfect original condition. $300.00-375.00. H. 6",
D. 6". Scroll bands and punched dots.

Butter, Apricots with Honeycomb (Looks like snakeskin)
$175.00-195.00. Good color; restored grip and handle.

Butter, Daisy and Trellis. $100.00-125.00. H. 6¾", D. 7". Restored bail and grip. **Butter, Dragonfly and Flower.** $95.00-110.00. Lid and handle missing. (hairline crack) H. 5", D. 8".

Butter, Dragonfly and Flower. Bail missing but with original lid fitting down securely over rim groove. $150.00-175.00. Pennsylvania Potter. H. 5½", D. 8".

Butter, Concave Roll Top, Blue Rings top and bottom. H. 4½", D. 8". $100.00-110.00. Lid disappeared.

Advertising Butter. $65.00-75.00. H. 6", D. 6". From a Dairy.

Two printed **Butter Crocks**, both all original: **Fancy** smaller H. 5″, D. 5″, with Victorian type medallion and lettering. **$125.00-150.00.** Larger **Printed** quite plain with a very substantial handle. **$100.00-125.00.**

Butter, Advertising. $150.00-175.00. H. 8″, D. 6½″. Deeply recessed lid; large ears; three-pound capacity; "RWS Co." on base is Red Wing Stoneware Co., Red Wing, Minnesota; Hazel Pure Food Company of Chicago has the signature of the company's President.

Butter (jar) Advertising.
$125.00-150.00. Extra-fine in
bailed Butter Containers. H. 7", D.
4". New wire, original grip; large
pulled ears; reverse side: "My Trade
Is What Quality Made".

Butter, Swastika.
$75.00-85.00. H. 5½", D.
6¼". See Page 79 for full
description and relation to
Indian Good Luck Sign; new
bail; scarcely-blue.

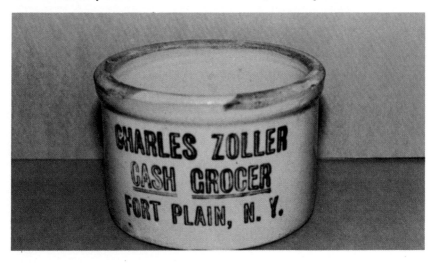

Butter, Advertising. $75.00-95.00. H. 4", D. 4½". Never had a lid;
printed information.

111

Spices and Storage (Canisters)

Snowflake, Six pieces in the set. **$110.00-125.00 each.** H. 6½ ″, D. 5¾ ″. Circa: 1900-1920. Maple wood lids with china knobs replace the original covers.

Diffused Blues, five pieces. **$100.00-110.00 each.** H. 6½ ″, D. 5¾ ″. New maple wood replacement lids.

Sets, Basketweave . . . pieces individually priced @ **$150.00 each up**. Self-explanatory labels of contents are on embossed unrolled scrolls; sets might also have had RICE and two more CEREALS; all have original clay tops intact - all plain knobs except for a flower finial on the **Cookie/Biscuit Jar**: that and the **Tobacco Jar** are 7½″ high; **Pepper, Allspice**, and others in the sets average 5″ high; the higher value is for mint (or nearly so) condition pieces as here.

Grooming, Comfort, and Sanitation

Bedpan, Diffused Blues. $100.00-115.00. H. 12″, Length 12″.

Chamber, Beaded Rose Cluster and Spear Points. $125.00-150.00. H. 6″, D. 9½″. Handle top shaped for better carrying convenience.

Chamber, Open Rose and Spear Point Panels. $100.00-115.00. H. 6″, D. 9½″. Heavy color on low relief flower causing a blurred design.

Chamber, Blueband with Earthworms (as named by collector-owner).
$310.00-325.00. H. 6″, D. 9½″. Tracery at top of rolled-out top.

Chamber, Wildflower. $100.00-125.00. Stenciled pattern. H. 6″, D. 11″.
Petal scallops background; blue-daubed inside rim and on applied handle.

Chamberpots (Waste Jars, Combinettes)

Chamberpot, Fleur de Lis and Scrolls. $200.00-225.00. H. 13", D. 10".
Original handle ends snapped into pulled out side ears.

Chamberpot, Bowknot. $125.00-145.00. H. 13", D. 10". The lid is a replacement, used because of its size. Known as a marriage, this practice of bringing together parts from separate old objects is fine if the owner is satisfied, and no harm in resale if the seller states it clearly. It's a matter of personal taste regarding completeness versus incompleteness.

Footwarmers

Diffused Blue Bands; mold mark down center of carrying handle. **$175.00-200.00.** Length 12½″, D. 6½″. Marked one end: **A Warm Friend,** the other: **Logan Pottery Co., Logan, Ohio;** Marked one side under the cork stopper: **Pat. Appl'd For.** Original cork stopper. It was asserted that hot water kept overnight in the Warmer could be poured our the next morning and ˙ be used still-warm for shaving.

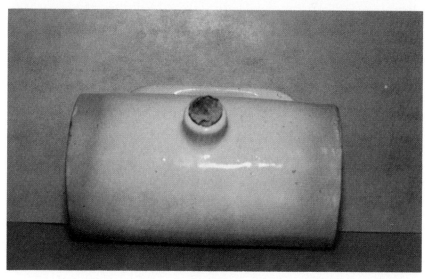

Two more **Footwarmers** from the Logan Pottery Co., Logan, Ohio; Few-of-a-size (that could be a Salesman's Sample or for carrying in a sleigh or even to church in frigid weather). Length 6″, Dia. 3½″. **Rare. $295.00-300.00.** Standard size **Footwarmer** from the same Logan pottery. **$150.00-175.00.** Diffused blue bands; each of these has the original cork stoppers; neither has the Pat. printing; Length 12½″, Dia. 3½″.

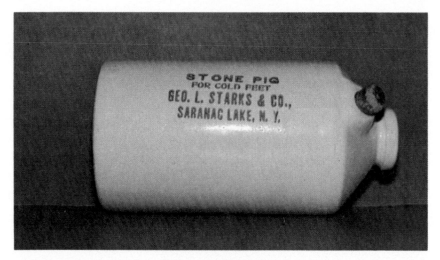

Footwarmer . . . **Stone Pig For Cold Feet. $195.00-250.00.** Length 11¼″, D. 5″. "GEO. L. STARKS & CO., SARANAC LAKE, N.Y." Not a commonly seen piece. Old cork "as found". No maker's mark - see Page 8.

"HENDERSON FOOT WARMER". $195.00-250.00. Length 12″, D. 5½″. Brass bushing (reinforcement around hole for brass cap "stopper"); imprinted at front base: "DORCHESTER POTTERY WORKS DORCHESTER, MASS." Circa: 1880.

Sand Jars

Sand Jars, Polar Bear . . .
B & W $275.00-300.00.
Brown $175.00-200.00.
Both H. 13½", D. 11".
Made in several sizes,
actually the Water Cooler
pattern minus it's spigot
and lid. Sometimes found
in brown, as shown here
with blue glazed interior,
and outside brushed-off-
color on figures. Used in
lobbies, foyers, etc. for
smokers to snuff out
glowing cigar butts, a step
toward public sanitation.

Spittoons (Cuspidors)

Spittoons (Cuspidors) . . . an effort at public cleanliness . . . made of glass, silver, brass, and tin as well as stoneware, popular from the 1840's, typical of taverns, hotels, railroad smoking cars (wherever people gathered), until by the 1860's they were accepted in some homes as "Parlor pieces".

Peacock. $250.00-275.00. H. 9″, D. 10″. Brick foundation design.

Poinsettia and Basketweave. $100.00-150.00. H. 9″, D. 9¾″. Blue glazed interior.

Sunflowers. $125.00-135.00. H. 9", D. 9¾".

Lilies & Plumes. $110.00-125.00. H. 9", D. 9¾".

Washstand Pieces

Pitcher and Bowl
Set, Feather and
Swirl.
$275.00-300.00.
Pitcher H. 12″, D.
8½″. Bowl H. 5″,
D. 14″.

Basketweave and Flower Set. $275.00-300.00. Pitcher H. 13″, D. 9″. Bowl
H. 4½″, D. 15″. "Pillowed"-edge bowl; spurred handle applied.

Fishscale and Wild Rose Set. $225.00-275.00. Pitcher H. 12½ " - Pitcher only **$150.00-175.00.** Bowl H. 4", D. 14". "Pleated"-edge bowl; flower in broken line medallion.

Toothbrush Holder, Blue Band. $50.00. H. 5½ ", D. 3¾ ". Rolled rim, good color.

·Set; 5 pieces, **Fishscale and Wild Roses. $400.00-450.00.** Large Hotwater Pitcher, Washbowl, smaller Pitcher for cooling water, Toothbrush Holder, Soap Dish. Rose patterns on many of the complete Washstand Sets are so often indistinct, almost smeared blues.

Hot Water Pitcher, Beaded Panels with Open Rose. $200.00-225.00. H.. 10″. D. 8″. Applied blue-daubed handle; squared top facilitates handling.

Hot Water Pitcher, Blue Band. $225.00-300.00. H. 12″, D. 9½″. Half-rim scallops with very high wide pouring lip pulled from the main form; an early piece. While this rim design is not commonly seen on stoneware, it was used on a pressed glass creamer and pitcher as early as an 1870's pattern, tankards seen circa: 1880's, an almost identical top from the U.S. Glass Company circa: 1913, and on a clear flint glass article now in the Sandwich Museum, circa: 1850.

Soap Dishes

Each is 4" to 5½" diameter, depth 1" to 1½"; all have embossed (raised) designs which, besides being ornamental, allowed moisture to ooze off the soap, after usage, into the straight or saucer-rimmed cavities. Used alone or with Washstand Sets, they are now heavily in demand.

Skillfully molded **Cat's Head**.
$130.00-165.00. Two excellently clear **Lion's Heads**, one with a benign expression, the other ferociously glaring.
$130.00-165.00 each.

Flower Cluster with Fishscale, flat dish center, walled edge.
$115.00-135.00. **Rose** in a Beaded Medallion. $115.00-125.00.
Embossed lines and saucer shaped dish.

Indian In War Bonnet. $150.00-175.00. In full regalia, framed by a bead-
ed snake; wall edge flat dish; much sought after.

Spongeware

Batter Jug. $195.00-225.00. H. 9″, D. 4½″. Uniquely fashioned; silky-sheer blue bands, deeply blue rim with recessed button finial lid; curved thick handle - note the inside of the separately molded applied handle was left unglazed, the clay grooved to prevent slipping when held; NO POUR-ING SPOUT - the thick batter pours perfectly without splashing . . . right onto the griddle.

Batter Jug. $195.00-225.00. H. 8″, D. 8″. Tiny thumb-pinched lip; the large mouth allows whipping or mixing the batter inside the Jug; the deep inside rim flange restrains thick (cornpone) batter from splashing while being mixed or poured into baking pans. (The owner had never seen a lid for this type Jug.)

Butter. $65.00-70.00.
H. 4″, D. 7″. Missing
lid; new wire handle.
Batter Jug (Pitcher)
Open. $150.00-175.00.
H. 6″, D. 5½″.
Pawprint Sponging;
thumb-pinched rim-lip;
mixing and pouring
piece.

Bean Pot (Crock). $250.00-275.00. BEANS printed near base. H. 8″, D.
8½″ widest part. Short-curved thick handle; made by Uhl Potter Co., Huntingburg, Indiana.

Bowl, Blue Rim, Random Dashes. $75.00-85.00. H. 2½″, D. 5½″.

Bowl, Mixing. $125.00-150.00. H. 3½″, D. 8″. Brush and sponge applications of good color and design.

Milk Bowl (Regionally a Crock). $75.00-115.00. H. 4″, D. 8″. Restored bail; could qualify as a stovetop piece.

Bowl, Berry, Mixing, Etc.
$100.00-125.00. H. 2¼", D.
6½". Brush-applied color rather
than sponge. Flat bottom
includes crock classification.

Milk Bowl (regionally a
Crock). **$125.00-150.00.**
H. 4½", D. 12".

Butter. $200.00-225.00. H.
5½", D. 6½". Word stencil
printed on plain clay
surrounded by a dot band;
lid has its own dropped
groove for inside-crock-
holding-without-slipping-off.

Mixing Bowl. $150.00-175.00. H. 6″, D. 13″. Rolled rim; most spongeware pieces have rim decorating, extending well over the inside edge or even as far as two inches and more.

Mixing (Dough) Bowl. $175.00-195.00. H. 5″, D. 14″. Wide rim collar; clear and blue bands.

Custard Bowl (Cup). **$75.00-100.00.** H. 3½″, D. 4″. Wide blue band; blues and oranges brush-decorating. **Cereal Bowl.** **$75.00-95.00.** H. 3½″, D. 4″. Blue and orange brush-applied colors. **Milk Crock** (Not spongeware). **$95.00-125.00.** No bail so not considered a stovetop piece. H. 5″, D. 8¾″. Impressed Star with radiant lines attributed to Star Stoneware Company of Akron, Ohio; unglazed exterior of soft pale-yellowish stoneware; interior is glazed a shiny-bright Robin's Egg blue.

Blue on Blue, Deeper Tones Against Paler Backgrounds

Salt Crock - not many of these. **$150.00-165.00.** H. 5½", D. 6¾". The lid groove is there but to date the collector had never seen one of the original lids. **Butter Pail. $125.00-150.00.** H. 5½", D. 5¾". Lid is missing.

Two **Butter Crocks (Jars). $95.00-100.00 each.** Each 5½", D. 5½". No original lids remaining - one bail gone.

Two **Blue on Blue Pitchers.** H. 9″, D. 6″. **$175.00-200.00.** H. 7″, D. 5½″. **$145.00-165.00.** Top and bottom grooving; pulled pointed spouts.

Pie Plate, Blue on Blue. $100.00 minimum. Dia. 10½″. Base view showing raised grooving for better kiln stacking and heat conduction while used in food baking; grayish but lighter than picture conveys.

Butter Crock (Jar).
$175.00-200.00. H. 5½", D.
6½". Not commonplace; mint
condition except for missing
snap-in bail. SWASTIKA
EMBLEM - See page 79 for
description.

Pitcher, Indian Good Luck Sign.
$150.00-175.00. H. 7", D. 7".
Reverse Swastika emblem embossed in raised frame; sponged
bands.

Chamber $200.00-225.00. Blue and White Lid Rings with what resembles
an attempt at a petal-ringaround body; H. 10", D. 10½"; interestingly
shaped body handle about the same size as that on the lid.

Cuspidor (Spittoon). $175.00-225.00. H. 10½″, D. 4″. Brass top fits over the pottery (for easier cleansing); was once in a St. Louis, Missouri bank lobby.

Meat Roaster, Woodland. $250.00-275.00. Uncommon piece, mint condition. H. 9″, D. 14″. Well balanced overall design; high finial; flat-bottomed good heat conductor.

Ice Bucket. **$135.00.** H. 6½", D. 6". New snap-in handle. **Creamer.**
$45.00-55.00. H. 3¾", D. 2½". **Mug. $65.00-75.00.** H. 4", D. 3¾".
Cup. $65.00-75.00. H. 3½", D. 3".

Four Mugs: Largest H. 6", D. 6". **$185.00-215.00.** Child-like rings from
a brush; rare piece. Three others are each: H. 4½", D. 2¾". **$85.00-100.00**
each. One has a daubed-on large blue spot on the bottom center - curious.

Pitcher, Blue on Blue. $150.00-175.00. H. 7", D. 5". Pitcher, Paneled Trees and Hills. $200.00-225.00. H. 12", D. 6". Note shaping of spout.

Pitcher, Grooved Bands. $225.00-250.00. H. 9", D. 7". Squared handle with knobs for convenient holding.

Pitcher, Pawprint. $150.00-165.00. H. 8¾", D. 6". Named because sponging resembles animal paw marks; a heavy pitcher with pulled lip. **Mug. $110.00-125.00.** H. 4", D. 4". **Pitcher, Navy Blues. $200.00-225.00.** H. 10", D. 6½". Grooving; step-out base for solid sitting without tipping.

Three **Bulbous (Bellied) Pitchers** from Uhl Pottery Company. Varying blues from very light to almost navy. H. 7", D. 3½" **$150.00-160.00.** H. 8½", D. 4½" **$175.00-185.00.** H. 10¼", D. 5" **$200.00-210.00.**

144

Soup Bowl . . . a rarity. **$175.00-195.00.** H. 2½", D. 6½". Interesting brush decorating, particularly on the inside-bowl walls. **Pitcher.** **$150.00-175.00.** Without cracked spout line value would be approximately $50.00 more. Tall pitchers are much admired. H. 10", D. 6½".

Pitcher, Ovoid. $125.00-150.00. Low-set top-spurred handle.

Tall Pitcher.
$225.00-250.00. H. 10", D. 6½".

Pitcher, Leaf and Flower.
$225.00-250.00. H. 10", D. 5". Embossed designs; lightly pinched spout; applied handle.

Pitcher, Flower Bands (also known as **Russian Milk Pitcher**) $175.00-200.00. H. 9″, D. 4″. **Pitcher, Flared Rim.** $150.00-175.00. H. 9″, D.4″; both Pitchers have continuing-rim pouring lips.

Dessert Plate, Cup and Saucer, Woven Band. $175.00-225.00 for 3 pcs. Plate D. 6½″. Brush-sponged with blue and red bands; brown flower ring; same design on all three pieces. A few small cinder ash points in glaze. Sponge treatment evident in the border as opposed to Spatterware - seeming almost "between" the two styles of decorating. Circa: latter 1800's.

Tankard. $375.00-395.00. H. 11½", D. 4½". "Step-in" top with a scarcely noticeable thumb-pinched pouring lip. A rare find.

Hot Water Pitcher, Ruffle Top. $300.00-350.00. H. 12", D. 7½". Graceful piece with wide blue band and flowers above it; large easy-pouring lip and wide graceful handle.

Soap Dish. $95.00-110.00.
Length 6", Width 4". Plain clay
center with raised bars so
moisture will drain off lathered
soap.

Soap Dish. $95.00-110.00.
Length 5½", H. 1". Cutout
patterned sides with three raised
bars to hold soap and permit
drying.

Crock. $75.00-85.00. H. 6", D. 5¼". **Syrup Jug. $310.00-365.00.** H. 6½",
D. 7" at widest part. Imprinted blue letters and ringaround; "GRAND-
MOTHER'S MAPLE SYRUP OF 50 YEARS AGO"; embossed underglaze
flowers; leaves at bail ears; "pulled" top back filler opening opposite the
applied (uncommon) pouring spout at front; separately molded top and bottom sections joined at noticeable center middle line.

149

Umbrella Stand (Holder). $375.00-450.00. H. 24″, D. 10″. A choice piece in any collection.

Index